50 Japanese Food Recipes for Home

By: Kelly Johnson

Table of Contents

- Sushi Rolls
- Miso Soup
- Teriyaki Chicken
- Tempura Vegetables
- Gyoza (Japanese Dumplings)
- Yakitori (Grilled Chicken Skewers)
- Tonkatsu (Breaded Pork Cutlet)
- Okonomiyaki (Japanese Pancake)
- Onigiri (Rice Balls)
- Ramen Noodles
- Udon Noodles
- Soba Noodles
- Chawanmushi (Savory Egg Custard)
- Karaage (Japanese Fried Chicken)
- Takoyaki (Octopus Balls)
- Donburi (Rice Bowl Dish)
- Sukiyaki (Japanese Hot Pot)
- Shabu-Shabu (Japanese Hot Pot)
- Oyakodon (Chicken and Egg Rice Bowl)
- Sashimi (Sliced Raw Fish)
- Okonomiyaki (Japanese Pancake)
- Taiyaki (Fish-Shaped Cake with Sweet Filling)
- Matcha Green Tea Ice Cream
- Anmitsu (Japanese Dessert with Jelly and Fruit)
- Dorayaki (Red Bean Pancake Sandwich)
- Katsu Curry (Curry with Breaded Pork Cutlet)
- Chirashi Sushi (Scattered Sushi)
- Zaru Soba (Cold Buckwheat Noodles)
- Yaki Onigiri (Grilled Rice Balls)
- Hiyayakko (Cold Tofu)
- Tamago Sushi (Egg Sushi)
- Nikujaga (Japanese Meat and Potato Stew)
- Omurice (Japanese Omelette Rice)
- Oden (Japanese Hot Pot)
- Tofu Dengaku (Grilled Tofu with Miso Glaze)

- Mitarashi Dango (Grilled Rice Dumplings with Sweet Soy Sauce)
- Tai Meshi (Sea Bream Rice)
- Korokke (Japanese Croquettes)
- Gomaae (Sesame Spinach)
- Buta no Kakuni (Braised Pork Belly)
- Yaki Udon (Stir-Fried Udon Noodles)
- Kakiage (Mixed Vegetable Tempura)
- Ankake Yakisoba (Yakisoba Noodles with Thick Sauce)
- Kinpira Gobo (Braised Burdock Root)
- Yudofu (Hot Tofu)
- Saba Shioyaki (Grilled Mackerel with Salt)
- Nasu Dengaku (Grilled Eggplant with Miso Glaze)
- Gyu Don (Beef and Onion Rice Bowl)
- Tamagoyaki (Japanese Rolled Omelette)
- Matcha Latte

Sushi Rolls

Ingredients:

- Sushi rice
- Nori (seaweed sheets)
- Fillings of your choice (e.g., cucumber, avocado, carrots, cooked shrimp, crab sticks, smoked salmon, etc.)
- Soy sauce, for serving
- Pickled ginger, for serving
- Wasabi, for serving

Instructions:

1. Cook sushi rice according to package instructions. Once cooked, let it cool slightly.
2. Place a sheet of nori shiny side down on a bamboo sushi mat or a clean kitchen towel.
3. Wet your hands with water to prevent sticking, then spread a thin layer of sushi rice evenly over the nori, leaving about 1-inch space at the top.
4. Arrange your desired fillings horizontally across the rice, closer to the bottom edge.
5. Start rolling the sushi tightly from the bottom edge using the mat or towel to help shape it. Apply gentle pressure as you roll to ensure it holds together.
6. Once rolled, use a sharp knife to slice the sushi roll into bite-sized pieces, wiping the knife with a damp cloth between cuts to prevent sticking.
7. Serve the sushi rolls with soy sauce, pickled ginger, and wasabi on the side for dipping.

Feel free to experiment with different fillings and combinations to create your favorite sushi rolls!

Miso Soup

Ingredients:

- 4 cups dashi stock (Japanese soup stock, can be made from kombu seaweed and bonito flakes)
- 3 tablespoons miso paste (white or red, to taste)
- 1/2 block tofu, diced into small cubes
- 2 green onions, thinly sliced
- 1 sheet nori (seaweed), cut into thin strips (optional)
- Optional additions: sliced mushrooms, wakame seaweed, thinly sliced vegetables like carrots or spinach

Instructions:

1. In a medium saucepan, bring the dashi stock to a gentle simmer over medium heat.
2. In a small bowl, mix a ladleful of the hot stock with the miso paste to dissolve it and create a smooth mixture.
3. Add the diluted miso paste back into the saucepan with the simmering stock and stir well to combine.
4. Add the diced tofu and any optional additions to the soup and let simmer for another 2-3 minutes until heated through.
5. Remove the soup from heat and stir in most of the sliced green onions, reserving some for garnish.
6. Ladle the miso soup into serving bowls and garnish with remaining green onions and nori strips, if using.
7. Serve hot and enjoy your homemade miso soup!

Feel free to adjust the amount of miso paste according to your taste preferences. Miso soup is versatile, so feel free to add other ingredients you like!

Teriyaki Chicken

Ingredients:

- 4 boneless, skinless chicken breasts or thighs
- 1/4 cup soy sauce
- 1/4 cup mirin (Japanese sweet rice wine)
- 2 tablespoons sake (Japanese rice wine) or dry sherry
- 2 tablespoons brown sugar or honey
- 2 cloves garlic, minced
- 1 teaspoon grated ginger
- 1 tablespoon vegetable oil
- Sesame seeds and sliced green onions, for garnish (optional)

Instructions:

1. In a bowl, mix together the soy sauce, mirin, sake, brown sugar or honey, minced garlic, and grated ginger to make the teriyaki sauce.
2. Place the chicken in a shallow dish or a resealable plastic bag. Pour half of the teriyaki sauce over the chicken, reserving the other half for later. Make sure the chicken is well coated in the sauce. Marinate in the refrigerator for at least 30 minutes, or up to 2 hours for more flavor.
3. Heat the vegetable oil in a large skillet or grill pan over medium-high heat. Once hot, add the chicken pieces, discarding any excess marinade. Cook the chicken for 6-8 minutes on each side, or until golden brown and cooked through, basting occasionally with the reserved teriyaki sauce.

4. Once the chicken is cooked through and caramelized, remove from the heat and let it rest for a few minutes.
5. Slice the chicken into thin strips or serve it whole. Garnish with sesame seeds and sliced green onions if desired.
6. Serve the teriyaki chicken hot with rice and steamed vegetables, and enjoy!

This homemade teriyaki chicken is deliciously sweet, savory, and perfect for a quick and easy weeknight meal.

Tempura Vegetables

Ingredients:

- Assorted vegetables of your choice (such as zucchini, sweet potato, bell pepper, broccoli, mushrooms, or green beans)
- 1 cup all-purpose flour
- 1/2 cup cornstarch
- 1 teaspoon baking powder
- 1/2 teaspoon salt
- 1 cup ice-cold water
- Vegetable oil, for frying
- Tempura dipping sauce (tentsuyu), for serving

Instructions:

1. Prepare the vegetables by cutting them into bite-sized pieces or slices. Make sure they are dry before dipping into the batter.
2. In a large bowl, combine the all-purpose flour, cornstarch, baking powder, and salt.
3. Gradually add the ice-cold water to the dry ingredients, whisking gently until just combined. Do not overmix; it's okay if the batter is slightly lumpy.
4. Heat vegetable oil in a deep frying pan or a pot to 350°F (180°C).
5. Dip the prepared vegetables into the batter, coating them evenly.
6. Carefully place the battered vegetables into the hot oil, making sure not to overcrowd the pan. Fry in batches if necessary.
7. Fry the vegetables for 2-3 minutes, or until they are golden brown and crispy.
8. Once cooked, remove the tempura vegetables from the oil using a slotted spoon or tongs, and transfer them to a plate lined with paper towels to drain any excess oil.
9. Serve the tempura vegetables hot with tempura dipping sauce (tentsuyu) on the side.
10. Enjoy your crispy and delicious tempura vegetables as a snack, appetizer, or as part of a meal!

Feel free to customize the vegetables according to your preferences, and don't forget to enjoy them while they're hot and crispy.

Gyoza (Japanese Dumplings)

Ingredients:

- 30 gyoza wrappers (round or square)
- 200g ground pork or chicken
- 1 cup finely shredded cabbage
- 2-3 green onions, finely chopped
- 2 cloves garlic, minced
- 1 tablespoon fresh ginger, grated
- 1 tablespoon soy sauce
- 1 tablespoon sesame oil
- 1/2 teaspoon sugar
- 1/4 teaspoon black pepper
- 1 tablespoon vegetable oil (for frying)
- Water, for sealing the dumplings

For the dipping sauce:

- 2 tablespoons soy sauce
- 1 tablespoon rice vinegar
- 1/2 teaspoon sesame oil
- Optional: chili oil or chili flakes, for heat

Instructions:

1. In a large mixing bowl, combine the ground pork or chicken, shredded cabbage, chopped green onions, minced garlic, grated ginger, soy sauce, sesame oil, sugar, and black pepper. Mix well until all ingredients are evenly incorporated.
2. To assemble the gyoza, place a small spoonful of the filling in the center of a gyoza wrapper. Dip your finger in water and moisten the edge of the wrapper. Fold the wrapper in half over the filling and pinch the edges together to seal, creating a half-moon shape. Pleat the edges if desired for a decorative finish. Repeat with the remaining wrappers and filling.

3. Heat vegetable oil in a large skillet or frying pan over medium heat. Once hot, arrange the gyoza in a single layer in the pan, making sure they're not touching each other. Cook for 2-3 minutes, or until the bottoms are golden brown.
4. Carefully pour water into the pan until it reaches about halfway up the sides of the gyoza. Immediately cover the pan with a lid to trap the steam. Let the gyoza steam for 5-7 minutes, or until the water has evaporated and the filling is cooked through.
5. While the gyoza are cooking, prepare the dipping sauce by mixing together soy sauce, rice vinegar, sesame oil, and chili oil or chili flakes if using.
6. Once the water has evaporated, remove the lid from the pan and continue cooking the gyoza for another minute or two, or until the bottoms are crisp and golden brown again.
7. Transfer the cooked gyoza to a serving plate and serve hot with the dipping sauce on the side.
8. Enjoy your homemade gyoza as a delicious appetizer or main dish!

Gyoza is best enjoyed fresh and hot, but you can also freeze uncooked gyoza for later use. Simply arrange them in a single layer on a baking sheet lined with parchment paper, then transfer to the freezer until frozen solid. Once frozen, you can transfer the gyoza to a freezer bag or container for storage. To cook frozen gyoza, follow the same instructions, but increase the cooking time slightly.

Yakitori (Grilled Chicken Skewers)

Ingredients:

- 500g boneless, skinless chicken thighs or chicken breast, cut into bite-sized pieces
- 4-5 green onions (scallions), cut into 2-inch pieces
- Yakitori sauce (tare):
    - 1/2 cup soy sauce
    - 1/4 cup mirin (Japanese sweet rice wine)
    - 1/4 cup sake (Japanese rice wine)
    - 2 tablespoons sugar
    - 2 cloves garlic, minced
    - 1 teaspoon grated ginger

Instructions:

1. If using bamboo skewers, soak them in water for at least 30 minutes to prevent them from burning during grilling.
2. In a small saucepan, combine all the ingredients for the yakitori sauce (soy sauce, mirin, sake, sugar, minced garlic, and grated ginger). Heat over medium heat, stirring occasionally, until the sugar has dissolved. Simmer for 5-7 minutes, or until the sauce has slightly thickened. Remove from heat and let it cool.
3. Thread the chicken pieces onto the skewers, alternating with pieces of green onion.
4. Preheat a grill or grill pan over medium-high heat. Brush the grill grates with oil to prevent sticking.
5. Place the skewers on the grill and cook for 3-4 minutes on each side, or until the chicken is cooked through and nicely charred, basting with the yakitori sauce occasionally during grilling.
6. Once the chicken is cooked through, remove the skewers from the grill and brush them with additional yakitori sauce for extra flavor.
7. Serve the yakitori skewers hot with steamed rice and extra yakitori sauce on the side for dipping.
8. Enjoy your homemade yakitori as a tasty appetizer or main dish!

Yakitori is incredibly versatile, so feel free to customize it with your favorite ingredients like mushrooms, bell peppers, or cherry tomatoes. Just remember to adjust the grilling time accordingly based on the ingredients you use.

Tonkatsu (Breaded Pork Cutlet)

Ingredients:

- 4 boneless pork loin chops, about 1/2 inch thick
- Salt and pepper, to taste
- 1/2 cup all-purpose flour
- 2 large eggs, beaten
- 1 cup panko breadcrumbs
- Vegetable oil, for frying
- Tonkatsu sauce (store-bought or homemade), for serving
- Shredded cabbage, for serving
- Cooked rice, for serving

Instructions:

1. Place each pork chop between two sheets of plastic wrap or parchment paper. Use a meat mallet or rolling pin to gently pound the pork chops until they are about 1/4 inch thick. Season both sides of the pork chops with salt and pepper.
2. Set up a breading station with three shallow bowls: one with flour, one with beaten eggs, and one with panko breadcrumbs.
3. Dredge each pork chop in the flour, shaking off any excess. Then dip it into the beaten eggs, allowing any excess to drip off. Finally, coat the pork chop in the panko breadcrumbs, pressing gently to adhere the crumbs.
4. Heat vegetable oil in a large skillet or frying pan over medium-high heat until it reaches about 350°F (175°C).
5. Carefully place the breaded pork chops into the hot oil, working in batches if necessary to avoid overcrowding the pan. Fry for 3-4 minutes on each side, or until the breading is golden brown and crispy and the pork is cooked through (reaches an internal temperature of 145°F or 63°C).
6. Once cooked, transfer the tonkatsu to a plate lined with paper towels to drain any excess oil.
7. Slice the tonkatsu into strips or pieces and serve hot with tonkatsu sauce, shredded cabbage, and cooked rice.
8. Enjoy your homemade tonkatsu as a delicious and satisfying meal!

Tonkatsu is often served with tonkatsu sauce, a thick and tangy Japanese sauce similar to Worcestershire sauce. You can find tonkatsu sauce in most Asian grocery stores, or you can make your own by combining ketchup, Worcestershire sauce, soy sauce, sugar, and a splash of sake or mirin. Adjust the ingredients to taste.

Okonomiyaki (Japanese Pancake)

Ingredients:

For the batter:

- 2 cups all-purpose flour
- 1 ½ cups dashi stock (can be substituted with water or chicken/vegetable stock)
- 2 large eggs
- 1 teaspoon soy sauce
- ½ teaspoon salt

For the filling (choose your favorites):

- 2 cups shredded cabbage
- 4 green onions, chopped
- 1 cup cooked protein (such as chopped cooked shrimp, sliced pork belly, or diced cooked chicken)
- Other optional additions: thinly sliced mushrooms, grated carrots, chopped squid, etc.

For topping:

- Okonomiyaki sauce (can be substituted with tonkatsu sauce or a mixture of Worcestershire sauce and ketchup)
- Japanese mayonnaise
- Aonori (dried seaweed flakes)
- Katsuobushi (dried bonito flakes)

Instructions:

1. In a large mixing bowl, whisk together the flour, dashi stock, eggs, soy sauce, and salt until smooth. The consistency should be similar to pancake batter. Adjust the amount of liquid if needed.

2. Add the shredded cabbage, chopped green onions, and any other fillings of your choice to the batter. Mix until well combined.
3. Heat a non-stick skillet or griddle over medium heat. Lightly oil the surface.
4. Pour a ladleful of the batter onto the skillet, spreading it out into a circle about 1/2 inch thick. You can make one large okonomiyaki or smaller individual ones.
5. Cook the okonomiyaki for 4-5 minutes on each side, or until golden brown and cooked through. Use a spatula to carefully flip it over.
6. Once both sides are cooked, transfer the okonomiyaki to a serving plate.
7. Drizzle okonomiyaki sauce and Japanese mayonnaise over the top of the pancake. Sprinkle with aonori and katsuobushi.
8. Repeat the process with the remaining batter and fillings.
9. Serve the okonomiyaki hot, cut into wedges, and enjoy!

Feel free to experiment with different fillings and toppings to create your favorite flavor combinations. Okonomiyaki is a versatile dish that can be adapted to suit your taste preferences.

Onigiri (Rice Balls)

Ingredients:

- 2 cups cooked Japanese sushi rice (short-grain rice)
- Salt
- Nori seaweed sheets, cut into thin strips (optional)
- Fillings of your choice (e.g., umeboshi plum, tuna mayo, cooked salmon, pickled vegetables, grilled chicken, etc.)

Instructions:

1. Let the cooked rice cool slightly until it's cool enough to handle but still warm.
2. Moisten your hands with water and sprinkle a little salt on your palms. This will prevent the rice from sticking to your hands and add flavor.
3. Take a handful of rice (about 1/2 cup) and place it in the palm of your hand. Flatten it slightly to form a small, oval-shaped mound.
4. Make an indentation in the center of the rice mound with your thumb.
5. Place a small amount of your chosen filling (about 1 teaspoon) into the indentation. Avoid overfilling, as it will make the onigiri difficult to shape and may cause it to fall apart.
6. Gently fold the rice over the filling, shaping it into a triangular or oval-shaped ball. Press firmly to compact the rice and ensure the filling is enclosed.
7. If desired, wrap a strip of nori seaweed around the outside of the onigiri to help hold its shape and add extra flavor. You can also leave the onigiri plain if you prefer.
8. Repeat the process with the remaining rice and filling ingredients.
9. Serve the onigiri immediately, or wrap them individually in plastic wrap to keep them fresh for later.

Onigiri can be enjoyed as a quick snack, packed lunch, or picnic food. They're also great for bento boxes or as a side dish with Japanese meals. Experiment with different fillings and shapes to create your favorite combinations!

Ramen Noodles

Ingredients:

For the broth:

- 6 cups chicken or vegetable broth
- 2 cloves garlic, minced
- 1 tablespoon fresh ginger, grated
- 2 tablespoons soy sauce
- 1 tablespoon mirin (Japanese sweet rice wine) or rice vinegar
- 1 tablespoon sesame oil
- Salt and pepper, to taste

For the toppings (choose your favorites):

- Cooked sliced pork or chicken
- Soft-boiled eggs, halved
- Sliced green onions
- Bamboo shoots
- Nori seaweed sheets, torn into pieces
- Corn kernels
- Bean sprouts
- Spinach
- Mushrooms (shiitake, enoki, or shimeji)

For the noodles:

- Fresh or dried ramen noodles (or you can use instant ramen noodles)
- Water for boiling

Instructions:

1. In a large pot, combine the chicken or vegetable broth, minced garlic, grated ginger, soy sauce, mirin or rice vinegar, and sesame oil. Bring to a simmer over medium heat. Season with salt and pepper to taste.
2. While the broth is simmering, prepare the toppings. Cook any protein you're using (pork, chicken, etc.) and slice it thinly. Soft-boil the eggs and slice them in half. Prepare any vegetables by slicing or chopping them as desired.
3. Cook the ramen noodles according to the package instructions. If using fresh ramen noodles, they typically cook in just a couple of minutes. Drain the noodles and rinse them under cold water to stop the cooking process and prevent them from becoming mushy.
4. Divide the cooked noodles among serving bowls. Arrange the cooked protein, soft-boiled eggs, sliced green onions, bamboo shoots, nori seaweed, and any other desired toppings on top of the noodles.
5. Ladle the hot broth over the noodles and toppings in each bowl. Make sure to distribute the broth evenly.
6. Serve the ramen noodles hot and enjoy!

Feel free to customize your ramen noodles with different toppings and adjust the broth's flavor according to your preferences. Homemade ramen is versatile and delicious, making it a perfect comfort food for any time of the year.

Udon Noodles

Ingredients:

For the noodles:

- 2 cups all-purpose flour
- 1/2 cup warm water
- 1/2 teaspoon salt

For the broth:

- 6 cups dashi stock (Japanese soup stock, can be made from kombu seaweed and bonito flakes)
- 1/4 cup soy sauce
- 2 tablespoons mirin (Japanese sweet rice wine)
- 2 tablespoons sake (Japanese rice wine)
- 1 tablespoon sugar
- Salt, to taste

Optional toppings:

- Sliced green onions
- Tempura flakes (tenkasu)
- Narutomaki (fish cake)
- Kamaboko (fish cake)
- Soft-boiled egg
- Sliced cooked chicken or beef
- Spinach or other leafy greens
- Wakame seaweed

Instructions:

1. To make the udon noodles, combine the all-purpose flour and salt in a large mixing bowl. Gradually add the warm water while stirring with a wooden spoon or chopsticks until a dough forms.
2. Knead the dough on a clean, floured surface for about 5-10 minutes, or until it becomes smooth and elastic. If the dough is too dry, add a little more water. If it's too sticky, add a little more flour.
3. Wrap the dough in plastic wrap and let it rest at room temperature for at least 30 minutes to allow the gluten to relax.
4. While the dough is resting, prepare the broth. In a large pot, combine the dashi stock, soy sauce, mirin, sake, and sugar. Bring to a simmer over medium heat. Taste and adjust the seasoning with salt if needed.
5. Divide the rested dough into 4 equal portions. Roll out each portion into a thin sheet, about 1/8 inch thick. Use a sharp knife or a pasta cutter to cut the dough into thick strips to form udon noodles.
6. Bring a large pot of water to a boil. Add the udon noodles and cook according to the package instructions, usually about 8-10 minutes for fresh noodles or 10-12 minutes for dried noodles. Stir occasionally to prevent sticking.
7. Once the noodles are cooked, drain them and rinse them under cold water to stop the cooking process and remove excess starch.
8. Divide the cooked udon noodles among serving bowls. Ladle the hot broth over the noodles, making sure to include some of the toppings if desired.
9. Serve the udon noodles hot, garnished with sliced green onions and any additional toppings you like.

Enjoy your homemade udon noodles as a comforting and satisfying meal!

Soba Noodles

Ingredients:

For the noodles:

- 2 cups buckwheat flour
- 1 cup all-purpose flour
- 1 cup water

For the dipping sauce (Tsuyu):

- 2 cups dashi stock (Japanese soup stock, can be made from kombu seaweed and bonito flakes)
- 1/2 cup soy sauce
- 1/4 cup mirin (Japanese sweet rice wine)
- 1 tablespoon sugar
- Optional: grated daikon radish and/or sliced green onions for garnish

Instructions:

1. In a large mixing bowl, combine the buckwheat flour and all-purpose flour.
2. Gradually add the water to the flour mixture while stirring with a fork or chopsticks until a dough forms.
3. Knead the dough on a clean, floured surface for about 5-10 minutes, or until it becomes smooth and elastic.
4. Wrap the dough in plastic wrap and let it rest at room temperature for at least 30 minutes to allow the gluten to relax.
5. While the dough is resting, prepare the dipping sauce (tsuyu). In a saucepan, combine the dashi stock, soy sauce, mirin, and sugar. Bring to a simmer over medium heat, then remove from heat and let it cool. Once cooled, transfer the dipping sauce to a serving bowl.
6. After the dough has rested, roll it out on a floured surface to a thickness of about 1/16 inch. Use a sharp knife or pasta cutter to cut the dough into thin strips to form soba noodles.

7. Bring a large pot of water to a boil. Add the soba noodles and cook according to the package instructions, usually about 5-7 minutes for fresh noodles or 8-10 minutes for dried noodles. Stir occasionally to prevent sticking.
8. Once the noodles are cooked, drain them and rinse them under cold water to stop the cooking process and remove excess starch.
9. Divide the cooked soba noodles among serving bowls. Serve the noodles with the dipping sauce (tsuyu) on the side for dipping.
10. Optional: Garnish the noodles with grated daikon radish and/or sliced green onions for extra flavor and texture.

Enjoy your homemade soba noodles as a delicious and nutritious meal!

Chawanmushi (Savory Egg Custard)

Ingredients:

- 2 cups dashi stock (Japanese soup stock, can be made from kombu seaweed and bonito flakes)
- 4 large eggs
- 1 tablespoon soy sauce
- 1 tablespoon mirin (Japanese sweet rice wine)
- 1/2 teaspoon salt
- Optional toppings: cooked shrimp, chicken, fish cake, shiitake mushrooms, ginkgo nuts, snow peas, etc.

Instructions:

1. Preheat your steamer over medium heat while you prepare the chawanmushi.
2. In a mixing bowl, whisk together the dashi stock, eggs, soy sauce, mirin, and salt until well combined.
3. Strain the egg mixture through a fine-mesh sieve to ensure a smooth texture.
4. Prepare your chawanmushi cups or small heatproof bowls by placing your desired toppings in the bottom of each cup.
5. Pour the strained egg mixture into the cups, filling them almost to the top.
6. Cover each cup tightly with plastic wrap or aluminum foil to prevent water from dripping into the custard during steaming.
7. Place the cups in the steamer basket, making sure they are not touching each other.
8. Steam the chawanmushi for about 15-20 minutes, or until the custard is set and no longer jiggles when shaken gently.
9. Once cooked, remove the chawanmushi from the steamer and let them cool slightly before serving.
10. Garnish the chawanmushi with additional toppings if desired, such as a sprinkle of chopped green onions or a drizzle of soy sauce.
11. Serve the chawanmushi warm as an appetizer or side dish, using a spoon to scoop out the custard from the cups.

Enjoy the delicate and savory flavors of homemade chawanmushi!

Karaage (Japanese Fried Chicken)

Ingredients:

- 500g boneless, skinless chicken thighs or breast, cut into bite-sized pieces
- 3 tablespoons soy sauce
- 2 tablespoons sake (Japanese rice wine) or dry sherry
- 1 tablespoon grated ginger
- 2 cloves garlic, minced
- 1 tablespoon sesame oil
- 1 tablespoon sugar
- 1/2 cup potato starch or cornstarch
- Vegetable oil, for frying
- Lemon wedges, for serving (optional)

Instructions:

1. In a mixing bowl, combine the soy sauce, sake, grated ginger, minced garlic, sesame oil, and sugar. Mix well to combine.
2. Add the chicken pieces to the marinade, making sure they are well coated. Cover the bowl and marinate the chicken in the refrigerator for at least 30 minutes, or up to 2 hours for more flavor.
3. Remove the marinated chicken from the refrigerator and let it sit at room temperature for about 10 minutes before frying.
4. Heat vegetable oil in a deep fryer or large skillet to 350°F (180°C).
5. Place the potato starch or cornstarch in a shallow dish. Coat each piece of marinated chicken in the starch, shaking off any excess.
6. Carefully add the coated chicken pieces to the hot oil in batches, making sure not to overcrowd the fryer or skillet. Fry for about 5-6 minutes, or until the chicken is golden brown and crispy, and cooked through.
7. Once cooked, remove the karaage from the oil using a slotted spoon and transfer them to a plate lined with paper towels to drain any excess oil.
8. Serve the karaage hot, with lemon wedges on the side for squeezing over the chicken if desired.

Enjoy your homemade karaage as a delicious appetizer, snack, or main dish served with rice and vegetables!

Takoyaki (Octopus Balls)

Ingredients:

- 1 1/2 cups all-purpose flour
- 2 cups dashi stock (Japanese soup stock, can be made from kombu seaweed and bonito flakes)
- 2 large eggs
- 1/2 teaspoon salt
- 1 tablespoon soy sauce
- 1/2 teaspoon baking powder
- 1/2 cup chopped cooked octopus (or substitute with cooked shrimp, crab, or other seafood)
- 1/4 cup chopped green onions
- 1/4 cup tenkasu (tempura scraps) or panko breadcrumbs
- Takoyaki sauce (store-bought or homemade)
- Japanese mayonnaise
- Aonori (dried seaweed flakes)
- Katsuobushi (dried bonito flakes)
- Pickled ginger (beni shoga), for serving (optional)

Takoyaki pan (a special pan with half-spherical molds)

Instructions:

1. In a large mixing bowl, combine the all-purpose flour, dashi stock, eggs, salt, soy sauce, and baking powder. Whisk until the batter is smooth.
2. Heat the takoyaki pan over medium heat and lightly oil the molds with vegetable oil or cooking spray.
3. Pour the batter into each mold, filling them about three-quarters full.
4. Add a small piece of chopped octopus, some chopped green onions, and a sprinkle of tenkasu or panko breadcrumbs into each mold.
5. As the batter starts to cook around the edges, use a skewer or takoyaki pick to gently push and rotate the edges towards the center, forming a ball shape.
6. Continue rotating and shaping the takoyaki balls as they cook, until they are evenly browned and crispy on the outside, and cooked through on the inside.
7. Once cooked, transfer the takoyaki balls to a serving plate.

8. Drizzle takoyaki sauce and Japanese mayonnaise over the top of the takoyaki balls. Sprinkle with aonori and katsuobushi.
9. Serve the takoyaki hot, garnished with pickled ginger if desired.

Enjoy your homemade takoyaki as a delicious and fun snack or appetizer!

Donburi (Rice Bowl Dish)

Ingredients:

For the rice:

- 2 cups Japanese short-grain rice
- 2 cups water

For the toppings (choose your favorites):

- Sliced cooked beef (gyudon)
- Sliced cooked chicken (oyakodon)
- Sliced cooked pork (butadon)
- Sliced cooked seafood (seafood donburi)
- Tofu (vegetarian option)
- Cooked vegetables (such as carrots, onions, mushrooms, spinach, etc.)

For the sauce:

- 1/4 cup soy sauce
- 2 tablespoons mirin (Japanese sweet rice wine)
- 1 tablespoon sugar
- 1 tablespoon sake (Japanese rice wine)
- 1 teaspoon grated ginger
- 1 teaspoon grated garlic

Optional garnishes:

- Sliced green onions
- Pickled ginger (beni shoga)
- Sesame seeds
- Nori seaweed flakes

Instructions:

1. Rinse the Japanese short-grain rice in a fine-mesh sieve under cold water until the water runs clear. Drain well.
2. In a rice cooker or a medium saucepan, combine the rinsed rice and water. Cook the rice according to the manufacturer's instructions for your rice cooker, or bring the rice and water to a boil in the saucepan, then reduce the heat to low, cover, and simmer for about 15-20 minutes, or until the rice is tender and the water is absorbed.
3. While the rice is cooking, prepare the sauce. In a small saucepan, combine the soy sauce, mirin, sugar, sake, grated ginger, and grated garlic. Bring the mixture to a simmer over medium heat, then reduce the heat to low and simmer for a few minutes until slightly thickened. Remove from heat and set aside.
4. Prepare the toppings by slicing and cooking the meat, seafood, tofu, and vegetables as desired. Keep warm until ready to serve.
5. Once the rice is cooked, fluff it with a fork and divide it among serving bowls.
6. Arrange the cooked toppings over the rice in each bowl.
7. Drizzle the sauce over the toppings and rice in each bowl.
8. Garnish the donburi with sliced green onions, pickled ginger, sesame seeds, and nori seaweed flakes if desired.
9. Serve the donburi hot and enjoy!

Donburi is a versatile dish, so feel free to customize it with your favorite ingredients and toppings. It's perfect for a quick and satisfying meal any time of the day!

Sukiyaki (Japanese Hot Pot)

Ingredients:

- 1 pound thinly sliced beef (such as ribeye or sirloin)
- 1/2 cup soy sauce
- 1/2 cup mirin (Japanese sweet rice wine)
- 1/4 cup sugar
- 1 cup dashi stock (Japanese soup stock, can be made from kombu seaweed and bonito flakes)
- 1 block firm tofu, sliced
- 1 bunch spinach, trimmed and washed
- 1/2 Napa cabbage, sliced
- 4-6 shiitake mushrooms, sliced
- 1 onion, thinly sliced
- 2-3 green onions, cut into 2-inch pieces
- 1 cup shirataki noodles (optional)
- 4-6 shirataki tofu noodles (optional)
- 2 tablespoons vegetable oil
- Cooked Japanese rice, for serving

Instructions:

1. In a large skillet or sukiyaki pot, heat vegetable oil over medium heat. Add the thinly sliced beef and cook until browned.
2. In a small bowl, mix together soy sauce, mirin, sugar, and dashi stock to make the sukiyaki sauce. Pour the sauce over the beef in the skillet.
3. Add sliced tofu, spinach, Napa cabbage, shiitake mushrooms, onion, and green onions to the skillet, arranging them evenly around the beef.
4. If using shirataki noodles, drain and rinse them under cold water. Add them to the skillet as well.
5. Cover the skillet and simmer for 5-7 minutes, or until the vegetables are tender and the beef is cooked through.
6. Serve sukiyaki hot directly from the skillet at the table. Each person can use chopsticks to pick ingredients from the skillet and dip them into a small bowl of beaten raw egg before eating. Alternatively, you can serve the sukiyaki with cooked Japanese rice on the side.

7. Enjoy the delicious and comforting flavors of homemade sukiyaki with your family and friends!

Sukiyaki is a communal dish that's perfect for sharing and enjoying together. Feel free to customize the ingredients and adjust the seasoning according to your preferences.

Shabu-Shabu (Japanese Hot Pot)

Ingredients:

For the broth:

- 6 cups water
- 2 cups dashi stock (Japanese soup stock, can be made from kombu seaweed and bonito flakes)
- 1/4 cup soy sauce
- 1/4 cup mirin (Japanese sweet rice wine)
- 2 tablespoons sake (Japanese rice wine)
- 2 cloves garlic, crushed
- 1-inch piece of ginger, sliced
- 2 green onions, cut into 2-inch pieces
- 1 tablespoon sugar
- Salt and pepper, to taste

For the hot pot:

- Thinly sliced meat (beef, pork, or chicken)
- Assorted vegetables (such as Napa cabbage, spinach, mushrooms, carrots, and tofu)
- Cooked udon noodles or rice noodles (optional)

For the dipping sauce:

- 1/4 cup soy sauce
- 1/4 cup mirin (Japanese sweet rice wine)
- 1 teaspoon sesame oil
- 1 green onion, finely chopped (optional)

Instructions:

1. In a large pot or a shabu-shabu pot, combine water, dashi stock, soy sauce, mirin, sake, garlic, ginger, green onions, sugar, salt, and pepper. Bring the broth to a simmer over medium heat.
2. While the broth is simmering, prepare the dipping sauce by combining soy sauce, mirin, sesame oil, and chopped green onions in a small bowl. Mix well and set aside.
3. Arrange thinly sliced meat, assorted vegetables, and cooked noodles on separate plates around the dining table.
4. Once the broth is simmering, place a few pieces of meat in a shabu-shabu basket or use chopsticks to cook the meat directly in the broth. Swirl the meat in the hot broth for a few seconds until it's cooked to your liking (the name "shabu-shabu" comes from the sound of swishing the meat in the hot broth). Remove the cooked meat from the broth and dip it into the dipping sauce before eating.
5. Repeat the process with the vegetables and noodles, cooking them in the hot broth until tender.
6. Continue cooking and enjoying the meat, vegetables, and noodles in the hot pot until all ingredients are cooked and eaten.
7. Once you've finished cooking, you can add more ingredients to the broth and continue enjoying shabu-shabu, or you can finish the meal with a serving of rice or udon noodles cooked in the flavorful broth.
8. Enjoy the delicious and interactive dining experience of homemade shabu-shabu with your family and friends!

Oyakodon (Chicken and Egg Rice Bowl)

Ingredients:

- 2 boneless, skinless chicken thighs, thinly sliced
- 1 onion, thinly sliced
- 3-4 large eggs
- 1 cup dashi stock (Japanese soup stock, can be made from kombu seaweed and bonito flakes)
- 3 tablespoons soy sauce
- 2 tablespoons mirin (Japanese sweet rice wine)
- 1 tablespoon sugar
- Cooked Japanese rice, for serving
- Sliced green onions, for garnish (optional)

Instructions:

1. In a medium-sized skillet or frying pan, combine dashi stock, soy sauce, mirin, and sugar. Bring the mixture to a simmer over medium heat.
2. Add sliced chicken thighs and onion to the simmering broth. Cook until the chicken is cooked through and the onion is softened, about 5-7 minutes.
3. In a separate bowl, beat the eggs lightly with a fork or chopsticks.
4. Once the chicken is cooked, reduce the heat to low and pour the beaten eggs evenly over the chicken and onion in the skillet.
5. Cover the skillet and let the eggs cook for 2-3 minutes, or until they are set but still slightly runny.
6. Remove the skillet from heat and let it sit, covered, for another minute to allow the residual heat to finish cooking the eggs.
7. To serve, divide the cooked rice among serving bowls. Carefully spoon the chicken, onion, and egg mixture over the rice, making sure to evenly distribute the broth.
8. Garnish with sliced green onions if desired.
9. Serve Oyakodon hot and enjoy!

Oyakodon is a comforting and satisfying meal that's perfect for a quick and easy dinner. Feel free to customize the dish by adding other ingredients such as mushrooms or green peas, and adjust the seasoning to your taste preferences.

Sashimi (Sliced Raw Fish)

Ingredients:

- Fresh fish fillets (common choices include tuna, salmon, yellowtail, mackerel, and halibut)
- Wasabi paste (optional)
- Soy sauce (for dipping)
- Pickled ginger (optional, for cleansing the palate)

Instructions:

1. Start by selecting the freshest fish available. It's essential to purchase fish specifically labeled as sushi-grade or sashimi-grade, which ensures it has been handled and stored properly for raw consumption.
2. Use a sharp chef's knife or a sashimi knife to slice the fish into thin, uniform pieces. Hold the knife at a slight angle and make smooth, gentle cuts across the grain of the fish. The thickness of the slices can vary depending on personal preference, but they are typically around 1/4 to 1/2 inch thick.
3. Arrange the sliced fish neatly on a plate, garnishing with thinly sliced cucumber, radish, or shiso leaves if desired.
4. Serve the sashimi immediately, accompanied by small bowls of soy sauce and wasabi paste for dipping. Pickled ginger can also be served on the side to cleanse the palate between bites.
5. Enjoy the delicate flavors and textures of fresh sashimi as a light and elegant appetizer or main course.

It's important to handle raw fish with care to prevent contamination and ensure food safety. Always store raw fish properly in the refrigerator and consume it as soon as possible after purchase. If you're unsure about preparing sashimi at home, consider purchasing it from a reputable sushi restaurant or fish market where it's prepared by trained professionals.

Okonomiyaki (Japanese Pancake)

Ingredients:

For the batter:

- 1 cup all-purpose flour
- 1 cup dashi stock (Japanese soup stock, can be made from kombu seaweed and bonito flakes)
- 2 large eggs
- 1/2 teaspoon salt
- 2 cups shredded cabbage
- 2 green onions, thinly sliced
- Optional: other fillings such as sliced pork belly, shrimp, squid, or vegetables like grated carrot, chopped mushrooms, etc.

For the toppings:

- Okonomiyaki sauce (store-bought or homemade)
- Japanese mayonnaise
- Aonori (dried seaweed flakes)
- Katsuobushi (dried bonito flakes)

Instructions:

1. In a large mixing bowl, whisk together the flour, dashi stock, eggs, and salt until smooth.
2. Add the shredded cabbage, sliced green onions, and any other fillings you're using to the batter. Mix until well combined.
3. Heat a non-stick skillet or griddle over medium heat. Lightly oil the surface.
4. Pour a ladleful of the batter onto the skillet, spreading it out into a circle about 1/2 inch thick. If using sliced pork belly or other meats, place them on top of the batter at this point.
5. Cook the okonomiyaki for 4-5 minutes on each side, or until golden brown and cooked through. Use a spatula to carefully flip it over.
6. Once both sides are cooked, transfer the okonomiyaki to a serving plate.

7. Drizzle okonomiyaki sauce and Japanese mayonnaise over the top of the pancake. Sprinkle with aonori and katsuobushi.
8. Serve the okonomiyaki hot, cut into wedges, and enjoy!

Feel free to customize your okonomiyaki with different fillings and toppings to suit your taste preferences. Okonomiyaki is a versatile and delicious dish that's perfect for a casual meal or snack.

Taiyaki (Fish-Shaped Cake with Sweet Filling)

Ingredients:

For the batter:

- 1 cup all-purpose flour
- 1 tablespoon cornstarch
- 1/4 teaspoon baking powder
- 2 tablespoons granulated sugar
- 1 large egg
- 3/4 cup milk
- 1 tablespoon melted butter or vegetable oil
- Vegetable oil or cooking spray for greasing the taiyaki mold

For the filling:

- Red bean paste (anko)
- Custard (you can use store-bought custard or make your own)
- Chocolate spread or Nutella (optional)

Instructions:

1. In a large mixing bowl, whisk together the all-purpose flour, cornstarch, baking powder, and granulated sugar.
2. In a separate bowl, beat the egg and then add the milk and melted butter or vegetable oil. Mix well.
3. Gradually pour the wet ingredients into the dry ingredients, stirring until smooth and well combined. The batter should be thick but pourable. If it's too thick, you can add a little more milk to thin it out.
4. Preheat your taiyaki mold on the stovetop over medium heat. Lightly grease the mold with vegetable oil or cooking spray.
5. Pour a small ladleful of batter into each side of the taiyaki mold, filling them about halfway.
6. Add a spoonful of your desired filling (red bean paste, custard, or chocolate spread) into the center of one side of the batter in each mold.

7. Close the taiyaki mold and cook for 2-3 minutes, or until the batter is set and golden brown.
8. Carefully flip the taiyaki mold over and cook for an additional 2-3 minutes on the other side, or until both sides are golden brown and crispy.
9. Once cooked, carefully remove the taiyaki from the mold and transfer them to a wire rack to cool slightly.
10. Serve the taiyaki warm and enjoy the deliciously sweet and crispy treats!

You can get creative with the fillings and toppings for your taiyaki, such as adding chocolate chips, fruit preserves, or even savory fillings like cheese or sausage.

Experiment with different flavors to find your favorite combination!

Matcha Green Tea Ice Cream

Ingredients:

- 2 cups heavy cream
- 1 cup whole milk
- 2/3 cup granulated sugar
- 3 tablespoons matcha green tea powder
- 4 large egg yolks
- 1 teaspoon vanilla extract
- Pinch of salt

Instructions:

1. In a medium saucepan, combine the heavy cream, whole milk, and granulated sugar. Heat the mixture over medium heat, stirring occasionally, until it begins to steam and small bubbles form around the edges. Do not let it boil.
2. In a separate bowl, whisk together the matcha green tea powder and egg yolks until smooth.
3. Gradually pour a small amount of the hot cream mixture into the matcha egg mixture, whisking constantly to temper the eggs. Continue to slowly add the hot cream mixture, whisking constantly, until fully combined.
4. Pour the mixture back into the saucepan and return it to the stove over medium-low heat. Cook, stirring constantly, until the mixture thickens slightly and coats the back of a spoon, about 5-7 minutes. Do not let it boil.
5. Remove the saucepan from the heat and stir in the vanilla extract and a pinch of salt.
6. Strain the mixture through a fine-mesh sieve into a clean bowl to remove any lumps or clumps.
7. Cover the bowl with plastic wrap, pressing it directly onto the surface of the mixture to prevent a skin from forming. Chill the mixture in the refrigerator for at least 4 hours or overnight until completely cold.
8. Once chilled, pour the mixture into an ice cream maker and churn according to the manufacturer's instructions until it reaches a soft-serve consistency.
9. Transfer the churned ice cream to a freezer-safe container and freeze for at least 4 hours or until firm.
10. Serve the matcha green tea ice cream scooped into bowls or cones, and enjoy!

Feel free to garnish your matcha green tea ice cream with additional matcha powder, whipped cream, or shaved chocolate for extra flavor and presentation.

Anmitsu (Japanese Dessert with Jelly and Fruit)

Ingredients:

For the agar jelly:

- 2 cups water
- 1 tablespoon agar agar powder
- 1/4 cup granulated sugar

For the sweet azuki bean paste (anko):

- 1 cup cooked sweetened azuki beans (canned or homemade)
- 1-2 tablespoons sugar (optional, adjust to taste)

For the syrup:

- 1/2 cup water
- 1/4 cup granulated sugar

For serving:

- Assorted fruits (such as strawberries, kiwi, pineapple, mandarin oranges, etc.), sliced or cubed
- Shiratama dango (sweet rice dumplings, optional)
- Ice cream (optional)
- Toasted sesame seeds (optional)
- Green tea (for serving)

Instructions:

1. Prepare the agar jelly: In a saucepan, combine water, agar agar powder, and granulated sugar. Bring the mixture to a boil over medium heat, stirring constantly

until the agar agar powder and sugar are completely dissolved. Remove from heat and pour the mixture into a shallow dish or mold. Let it cool and set in the refrigerator for at least 1 hour, then cut it into cubes.
2. Prepare the sweet azuki bean paste (anko): If using canned azuki beans, drain and rinse them. If using homemade beans, cook them according to package instructions, then sweeten with sugar to taste. Mash the beans into a paste-like consistency.
3. Prepare the syrup: In a small saucepan, combine water and granulated sugar. Bring the mixture to a boil over medium heat, stirring until the sugar is completely dissolved. Remove from heat and let it cool.
4. Assemble the Anmitsu: Divide the agar jelly cubes, sweet azuki bean paste, and assorted fruits among serving bowls. Optionally, add shiratama dango and a scoop of ice cream. Sprinkle with toasted sesame seeds if desired.
5. Drizzle the syrup over the Anmitsu.
6. Serve the Anmitsu with a side of green tea for a traditional Japanese dessert experience.

Feel free to customize your Anmitsu with your favorite fruits and toppings. It's a versatile dessert that can be enjoyed year-round!

Dorayaki (Red Bean Pancake Sandwich)

Ingredients:

For the pancakes:

- 2 large eggs
- 1/2 cup granulated sugar
- 1 tablespoon honey
- 1 teaspoon vanilla extract
- 1 cup all-purpose flour
- 1 teaspoon baking powder
- 2-3 tablespoons water (if needed)
- Vegetable oil for cooking

For the filling:

- Sweetened red bean paste (anko)

Instructions:

1. In a mixing bowl, whisk together the eggs, granulated sugar, honey, and vanilla extract until well combined.
2. Sift the all-purpose flour and baking powder into the egg mixture. Mix until smooth. If the batter is too thick, add water, 1 tablespoon at a time, until you reach a pourable consistency.
3. Heat a non-stick skillet or griddle over medium heat. Lightly grease the surface with vegetable oil.
4. Pour about 1/4 cup of the pancake batter onto the skillet, spreading it out into a circle about 3-4 inches in diameter.
5. Cook the pancake for 1-2 minutes, or until bubbles form on the surface and the edges begin to set.
6. Flip the pancake and cook for an additional 1-2 minutes, or until golden brown on both sides and cooked through.
7. Repeat with the remaining batter, greasing the skillet as needed.
8. Once all the pancakes are cooked, let them cool slightly.

9. To assemble the Dorayaki, spread a spoonful of sweetened red bean paste onto the center of one pancake. Place another pancake on top, pressing gently to sandwich the filling.
10. Repeat with the remaining pancakes and filling.
11. Serve the Dorayaki at room temperature and enjoy!

Dorayaki is best enjoyed fresh, but you can store any leftovers in an airtight container at room temperature for up to 2 days or in the refrigerator for up to 1 week. Simply reheat them in the microwave or on a skillet before serving.

Katsu Curry (Curry with Breaded Pork Cutlet)

Ingredients:

For the tonkatsu:

- 4 boneless pork loin chops, about 1/2 inch thick
- Salt and pepper, to taste
- 1/2 cup all-purpose flour
- 2 large eggs, beaten
- 1 cup panko breadcrumbs
- Vegetable oil for frying

For the curry sauce:

- 2 tablespoons vegetable oil
- 1 onion, finely chopped
- 2 carrots, peeled and diced
- 2 potatoes, peeled and diced
- 2 cloves garlic, minced
- 2 tablespoons curry powder
- 2 tablespoons all-purpose flour
- 3 cups chicken or vegetable broth
- 2 tablespoons soy sauce
- 1 tablespoon Worcestershire sauce
- Salt and pepper, to taste

For serving:

- Cooked Japanese rice
- Thinly sliced cabbage or shredded lettuce
- Fukujinzuke (Japanese pickles), for garnish (optional)

Instructions:

1. Start by preparing the tonkatsu. Season the pork chops with salt and pepper on both sides.
2. Set up a breading station with three shallow bowls: one with flour, one with beaten eggs, and one with panko breadcrumbs.
3. Dredge each pork chop in the flour, shaking off any excess. Dip it into the beaten eggs, coating it evenly. Finally, coat the pork chop in panko breadcrumbs, pressing gently to adhere.
4. Heat vegetable oil in a large skillet or frying pan over medium-high heat. Fry the breaded pork chops for 3-4 minutes on each side, or until golden brown and cooked through. Transfer to a paper towel-lined plate to drain excess oil.
5. While the pork chops are frying, prepare the curry sauce. In a large saucepan or Dutch oven, heat vegetable oil over medium heat. Add the chopped onion, carrots, potatoes, and minced garlic. Cook, stirring occasionally, until the vegetables are softened.
6. Stir in the curry powder and flour, and cook for 1-2 minutes until fragrant.
7. Gradually pour in the chicken or vegetable broth, stirring constantly to prevent lumps from forming.
8. Add soy sauce, Worcestershire sauce, salt, and pepper to taste. Bring the mixture to a simmer and cook for 15-20 minutes, or until the vegetables are tender and the sauce has thickened.
9. Once the curry sauce is ready, remove it from heat and blend it using an immersion blender or transfer it to a regular blender and blend until smooth. Return the sauce to the pot and keep warm.
10. To serve, slice the tonkatsu into strips and place it on top of cooked Japanese rice. Ladle the curry sauce over the tonkatsu and rice. Garnish with thinly sliced cabbage or shredded lettuce and fukujinzuke, if desired.
11. Enjoy your homemade katsu curry!

Chirashi Sushi (Scattered Sushi)

Ingredients:

For the sushi rice:

- 2 cups sushi rice
- 2 cups water
- 1/4 cup rice vinegar
- 2 tablespoons granulated sugar
- 1 teaspoon salt

For the toppings (choose your favorites):

- Sashimi-grade fish (such as tuna, salmon, yellowtail, or shrimp), thinly sliced
- Cooked seafood (such as crab, shrimp, or scallops)
- Assorted vegetables (such as cucumber, avocado, radish, or carrot), thinly sliced or julienned
- Tamagoyaki (Japanese rolled omelette), sliced into strips
- Pickled ginger (gari), for garnish
- Wasabi paste, for serving
- Soy sauce, for serving

Instructions:

1. Rinse the sushi rice in a fine-mesh sieve under cold water until the water runs clear. Drain well.
2. In a rice cooker or a medium saucepan, combine the rinsed rice and water. Cook the rice according to the manufacturer's instructions for your rice cooker, or bring the rice and water to a boil in the saucepan, then reduce the heat to low, cover, and simmer for about 15-20 minutes, or until the rice is tender and the water is absorbed.
3. While the rice is cooking, prepare the sushi vinegar. In a small saucepan, heat the rice vinegar, granulated sugar, and salt over low heat, stirring until the sugar and salt are dissolved. Remove from heat and let it cool.

4. Once the rice is cooked, transfer it to a large mixing bowl. Gently fold in the sushi vinegar mixture, being careful not to mash the rice. Allow the seasoned rice to cool to room temperature.
5. Prepare the toppings by slicing or julienning the seafood, vegetables, and tamagoyaki.
6. To assemble the chirashi sushi, divide the seasoned sushi rice among serving bowls. Arrange the sliced or julienned toppings on top of the rice in an attractive pattern.
7. Garnish the chirashi sushi with pickled ginger (gari) and serve with wasabi paste and soy sauce on the side.
8. Enjoy your homemade chirashi sushi as a colorful and delicious meal that's perfect for any occasion!

Feel free to customize your chirashi sushi with your favorite ingredients and toppings.

It's a versatile dish that's as visually stunning as it is tasty!

Zaru Soba (Cold Buckwheat Noodles)

Ingredients:

For the soba noodles:

- 8 ounces dried soba noodles (buckwheat noodles)

For the dipping sauce (tsuyu):

- 1 cup dashi stock (Japanese soup stock, can be made from kombu seaweed and bonito flakes)
- 1/4 cup soy sauce
- 1/4 cup mirin (Japanese sweet rice wine)
- 1 tablespoon sugar
- Optional: grated daikon radish, thinly sliced green onions, wasabi paste, shredded nori seaweed, for garnish

Instructions:

1. Cook the soba noodles according to the package instructions. Bring a large pot of water to a boil, add the soba noodles, and cook for about 4-5 minutes, or until tender but still firm to the bite (al dente). Be careful not to overcook the noodles. Drain the noodles and rinse them under cold running water until they are cool. This helps remove excess starch and prevents them from sticking together.
2. While the noodles are cooking, prepare the dipping sauce (tsuyu). In a small saucepan, combine the dashi stock, soy sauce, mirin, and sugar. Bring the mixture to a simmer over medium heat, stirring occasionally, until the sugar is dissolved. Remove from heat and let the tsuyu cool to room temperature.
3. Once the soba noodles are cooked and cooled, divide them among serving plates or place them on a bamboo zaru (soba serving tray) if available.
4. Serve the soba noodles with the dipping sauce (tsuyu) in individual small bowls or cups.
5. Optionally, garnish the soba noodles with grated daikon radish, thinly sliced green onions, wasabi paste, and shredded nori seaweed.

6. To eat, take a small portion of soba noodles with chopsticks and dip them into the tsuyu sauce. Enjoy the refreshing taste and texture of cold zaru soba!

Zaru soba is a light and healthy dish that's perfect for hot summer days. Feel free to customize your zaru soba with additional toppings or serve it with tempura or other side dishes for a complete meal.

Yaki Onigiri (Grilled Rice Balls)

Ingredients:

- 2 cups cooked Japanese short-grain rice (preferably leftover rice)
- 1 tablespoon soy sauce
- 1 tablespoon mirin (Japanese sweet rice wine)
- Vegetable oil for brushing

Optional toppings:

- Nori seaweed strips
- Sesame seeds
- Furikake (Japanese rice seasoning)
- Bonito flakes (katsuobushi)
- Soy sauce or teriyaki sauce for brushing

Instructions:

1. In a mixing bowl, combine the cooked rice, soy sauce, and mirin. Mix well until the rice is evenly coated with the seasonings.
2. Divide the seasoned rice into equal portions and shape each portion into a compact triangle or ball shape. You can wet your hands with water to prevent the rice from sticking.
3. Preheat a grill or grill pan over medium heat. Lightly oil the grill grates or pan to prevent sticking.
4. Place the shaped rice balls on the grill and cook for about 3-4 minutes on each side, or until golden brown and crispy.
5. Optional: Brush the grilled rice balls with soy sauce or teriyaki sauce for added flavor.
6. Once the rice balls are cooked through and crispy on the outside, remove them from the grill and transfer them to a serving plate.
7. Optional: Garnish the yaki onigiri with nori seaweed strips, sesame seeds, furikake, or bonito flakes for extra flavor and presentation.
8. Serve the yaki onigiri hot as a delicious and satisfying snack or side dish.

Yaki onigiri is versatile and can be enjoyed on its own or paired with a variety of toppings and sauces. Get creative and customize your yaki onigiri with your favorite flavors and ingredients!

Hiyayakko (Cold Tofu)

Ingredients:

- 1 block of silken tofu
- 1 tablespoon soy sauce
- 1 teaspoon sesame oil (optional)
- 1 tablespoon finely chopped green onions
- 1 teaspoon grated ginger
- Bonito flakes (katsuobushi), for garnish (optional)
- Toasted sesame seeds, for garnish (optional)

Instructions:

1. Carefully remove the tofu from its packaging and drain any excess liquid. You can wrap the tofu block in a paper towel and gently press to remove more moisture if desired.
2. Cut the tofu block into individual serving portions. Traditionally, it's cut into cubes or rectangles.
3. Arrange the tofu pieces on serving plates or a serving dish.
4. In a small bowl, mix together the soy sauce and sesame oil (if using).
5. Drizzle the soy sauce mixture evenly over the tofu pieces.
6. Sprinkle the chopped green onions and grated ginger over the tofu.
7. Optionally, garnish with bonito flakes and toasted sesame seeds for added flavor and presentation.
8. Serve immediately and enjoy your refreshing Hiyayakko!

Feel free to adjust the toppings and seasonings according to your taste preferences.

You can also customize it with other toppings like shredded nori, shredded daikon radish, or chili oil for a spicy kick. Enjoy!

Tamago Sushi (Egg Sushi)

Ingredients:

For the Tamago (Egg):

- 4 large eggs
- 2 tablespoons granulated sugar
- 2 tablespoons mirin (Japanese sweet rice wine)
- 1 tablespoon soy sauce
- Vegetable oil for cooking

For the Sushi Rice:

- 1 cup sushi rice
- 1 1/4 cups water
- 2 tablespoons rice vinegar
- 1 tablespoon sugar
- 1/2 teaspoon salt

For Assembly:

- Nori sheets (optional, for wrapping)
- Soy sauce, wasabi, and pickled ginger for serving (optional)

Instructions:

1. Rinse the sushi rice in a fine mesh sieve under cold water until the water runs clear. Drain well.
2. In a rice cooker or saucepan, combine the rinsed rice and water. Cook according to the rice cooker's instructions or bring to a boil, then reduce the heat to low, cover, and simmer for about 15-20 minutes, or until the rice is tender and the water is absorbed.

3. While the rice is cooking, prepare the Tamago (egg). In a bowl, whisk together the eggs, sugar, mirin, and soy sauce until well combined.
4. Heat a non-stick frying pan over medium heat and lightly grease with vegetable oil. Pour a thin layer of the egg mixture into the pan, tilting the pan to spread the mixture evenly. Cook until the bottom is set but the top is still slightly runny.
5. Using a spatula, carefully roll up the cooked egg from one end of the pan to the other, creating a thin egg roll. Push the roll to one end of the pan and add more egg mixture to the empty side. Lift the rolled egg to allow the uncooked egg to flow underneath. Repeat this process until all the egg mixture is used and the egg roll is cooked through. Remove from heat and let it cool.
6. In a small saucepan, combine the rice vinegar, sugar, and salt. Heat over low heat until the sugar and salt dissolve. Remove from heat and let it cool slightly.
7. Once the rice is cooked, transfer it to a large bowl and gently fold in the seasoned vinegar mixture using a rice paddle or spatula. Be careful not to smash the grains of rice. Allow the rice to cool to room temperature.
8. Once the Tamago and sushi rice have cooled, slice the Tamago into thin rectangular slices.
9. To assemble the Tamago Sushi, take a small amount of sushi rice and shape it into an oval or rectangular mound using slightly wet hands. Place a slice of Tamago on top of the rice.
10. Optionally, wrap the Tamago sushi with a strip of nori seaweed, or leave it unwrapped.
11. Repeat the process until all the Tamago and sushi rice are used.
12. Serve the Tamago Sushi with soy sauce, wasabi, and pickled ginger on the side, if desired.

Enjoy your homemade Tamago Sushi!

Nikujaga (Japanese Meat and Potato Stew)

Ingredients:

- 400g thinly sliced beef (you can also use pork if you prefer)
- 3 medium potatoes, peeled and cut into chunks
- 1 large onion, thinly sliced
- 2 carrots, peeled and sliced
- 1 cup dashi stock (you can use instant dashi granules or make your own from kombu and bonito flakes)
- 3 tablespoons soy sauce
- 3 tablespoons mirin (Japanese sweet rice wine)
- 2 tablespoons sugar
- 1 tablespoon vegetable oil
- Salt to taste
- Chopped green onions for garnish (optional)

Instructions:

1. In a large pot or deep skillet, heat the vegetable oil over medium heat. Add the thinly sliced onion and cook until softened and translucent.
2. Add the thinly sliced beef to the pot and cook until browned, breaking up any large clumps with a spatula.
3. Once the beef is browned, add the potatoes and carrots to the pot.
4. In a separate bowl, mix together the dashi stock, soy sauce, mirin, and sugar until well combined. Pour this mixture over the beef and vegetables in the pot.
5. Bring the mixture to a boil, then reduce the heat to low and simmer, covered, for about 20-25 minutes, or until the potatoes and carrots are tender and cooked through.
6. Taste the Nikujaga and adjust the seasoning with salt if necessary.
7. Once the vegetables are cooked and the flavors have melded together, remove the pot from the heat.
8. Serve the Nikujaga hot, garnished with chopped green onions if desired. It's typically enjoyed with steamed rice and perhaps a side of pickles or other Japanese accompaniments.

Nikujaga is a versatile dish, so feel free to customize it to your liking by adjusting the ingredients or seasoning according to your taste preferences. Enjoy your homemade Nikujaga!

Omurice (Japanese Omelette Rice)

Ingredients:

For the Fried Rice:

- 2 cups cooked Japanese short-grain rice (preferably day-old)
- 1 tablespoon vegetable oil
- 1/2 onion, finely chopped
- 1 small carrot, finely diced
- 1/2 cup frozen peas
- 2 tablespoons ketchup
- Salt and pepper to taste

For the Omelette:

- 4 large eggs
- 1 tablespoon milk or water
- Salt and pepper to taste
- 1 tablespoon butter

For Garnish (optional):

- Additional ketchup
- Chopped green onions or parsley

Instructions:

1. Heat the vegetable oil in a large skillet or frying pan over medium heat. Add the chopped onion and cook until softened and translucent.
2. Add the diced carrot to the skillet and cook for a few minutes until it starts to soften.
3. Stir in the frozen peas and cook for another minute.

4. Add the cooked rice to the skillet, breaking up any clumps with a spatula. Stir-fry the rice with the vegetables until heated through.
5. Add the ketchup to the skillet and stir to coat the rice evenly. Season with salt and pepper to taste. Keep the fried rice warm while you prepare the omelette.
6. In a bowl, whisk together the eggs, milk (or water), salt, and pepper until well combined.
7. Heat the butter in a non-stick skillet over medium-low heat. Once the butter has melted and is foamy, pour the egg mixture into the skillet.
8. Allow the eggs to cook undisturbed for a minute or two until the bottom starts to set.
9. Gently push the cooked edges of the omelette towards the center of the skillet, tilting the skillet to allow the uncooked eggs to flow to the edges. Continue cooking until the eggs are mostly set but still slightly runny on top.
10. Spoon the fried rice onto one half of the omelette in the skillet.
11. Carefully fold the other half of the omelette over the fried rice to enclose it, forming a half-moon shape.
12. Slide the Omurice onto a plate, seam side down. If desired, drizzle additional ketchup on top and garnish with chopped green onions or parsley.
13. Serve the Omurice immediately and enjoy!

Omurice is a versatile dish, so feel free to customize it by adding other ingredients such as cooked chicken, ham, mushrooms, or bell peppers to the fried rice.

Oden (Japanese Hot Pot)

Ingredients:

For the Broth:

- 6 cups dashi stock (you can use instant dashi granules or make your own from kombu and bonito flakes)
- 1/4 cup soy sauce
- 2 tablespoons mirin (Japanese sweet rice wine)
- 1 tablespoon sake (Japanese rice wine)
- 1 tablespoon sugar
- Salt to taste

For the Oden Ingredients (you can mix and match based on your preferences):

- Daikon radish, peeled and cut into thick rounds
- Konnyaku (konjac), cut into bite-sized pieces
- Hard-boiled eggs, peeled
- Fish cakes (such as chikuwa, ganmodoki, or hanpen)
- Tofu, cut into cubes
- Japanese mustard (karashi) for serving (optional)

Instructions:

1. In a large pot, combine the dashi stock, soy sauce, mirin, sake, and sugar. Bring the mixture to a boil over medium heat.
2. Once the broth is boiling, reduce the heat to low and let it simmer for about 10-15 minutes to allow the flavors to meld together. Taste the broth and adjust the seasoning with salt if necessary.
3. While the broth is simmering, prepare the Oden ingredients. Cut the daikon radish, konnyaku, tofu, and any other ingredients into bite-sized pieces.
4. Add the daikon radish and konnyaku to the simmering broth first, as they take longer to cook. Let them simmer for about 15-20 minutes, or until they are tender.

5. Once the daikon radish and konnyaku are tender, add the remaining Oden ingredients to the pot. Let them simmer for another 10-15 minutes, or until they are heated through and infused with the flavors of the broth.
6. Once all the ingredients are cooked, ladle the Oden into individual serving bowls, making sure to distribute the various ingredients evenly.
7. Serve the Oden hot, along with Japanese mustard (karashi) on the side for dipping if desired.

Oden is often enjoyed as a one-pot meal on its own, but you can also serve it with steamed rice or as part of a larger Japanese meal. Feel free to adjust the ingredients and seasoning according to your taste preferences. Enjoy your homemade Oden!

Tofu Dengaku (Grilled Tofu with Miso Glaze)

Ingredients:

- 1 block of firm tofu (about 14-16 ounces)
- 2 tablespoons white miso paste
- 1 tablespoon mirin (Japanese sweet rice wine)
- 1 tablespoon sugar
- 1 tablespoon soy sauce
- 1 teaspoon sesame oil
- Optional toppings: toasted sesame seeds, chopped green onions, thinly sliced nori seaweed

Instructions:

1. Drain the tofu and wrap it in a clean kitchen towel or paper towels. Place a weight on top (such as a plate with a heavy can) to press out excess moisture. Let it press for about 15-30 minutes.
2. In the meantime, prepare the miso glaze. In a small saucepan, combine the white miso paste, mirin, sugar, soy sauce, and sesame oil. Cook over low heat, stirring constantly, until the sugar has dissolved and the mixture is smooth. Remove from heat and set aside.
3. Preheat your grill or broiler. If using a grill, lightly oil the grates to prevent sticking.
4. Cut the pressed tofu block into thick slices or cubes, depending on your preference.
5. Brush each side of the tofu slices with a little bit of oil to prevent sticking.
6. Grill or broil the tofu slices until they are lightly browned and have grill marks, about 4-5 minutes per side.
7. Once the tofu is cooked, brush a generous amount of the miso glaze onto each side of the tofu slices.
8. Return the glazed tofu to the grill or broiler and cook for an additional 1-2 minutes on each side, or until the glaze is caramelized and bubbly.
9. Remove the tofu from the heat and transfer to a serving plate.
10. Optionally, sprinkle toasted sesame seeds, chopped green onions, or thinly sliced nori seaweed on top for garnish.
11. Serve the Tofu Dengaku hot as an appetizer or part of a meal. It pairs well with steamed rice and a side of vegetables.

Enjoy your delicious homemade Tofu Dengaku!

Mitarashi Dango (Grilled Rice Dumplings with Sweet Soy Sauce)

Ingredients:

For the Dango:

- 1 cup mochiko (sweet rice flour)
- 1/2 cup water

For the Sweet Soy Sauce Glaze:

- 1/4 cup soy sauce
- 2 tablespoons sugar
- 1 tablespoon mirin (Japanese sweet rice wine)
- 1 tablespoon katakuriko (potato starch) or cornstarch
- 2 tablespoons water

For Skewering:

- Bamboo skewers

Instructions:

1. Start by making the dango. In a mixing bowl, combine the mochiko and water. Mix until a smooth dough forms. If the dough is too dry, add a little more water, and if it's too wet, add a bit more mochiko.
2. Divide the dough into small pieces and roll each piece into a ball about the size of a marble.
3. Bring a pot of water to a boil. Drop the dango balls into the boiling water and cook them until they float to the surface, about 2-3 minutes.
4. Remove the cooked dango balls from the boiling water using a slotted spoon and transfer them to a bowl of cold water to cool briefly. Drain the dango balls and set them aside.

5. Skewer the cooled dango balls onto bamboo skewers, usually 3-5 balls per skewer, depending on their size.
6. Preheat your grill or broiler.
7. While the grill or broiler is heating, prepare the sweet soy sauce glaze. In a small saucepan, combine the soy sauce, sugar, and mirin. Cook over medium heat until the sugar has dissolved.
8. In a separate bowl, mix the katakuriko or cornstarch with water to make a slurry. Add the slurry to the saucepan and stir well.
9. Cook the glaze, stirring constantly, until it thickens to a syrupy consistency. Remove from heat.
10. Grill or broil the skewered dango balls until they are lightly browned and have grill marks, about 1-2 minutes per side.
11. Once the dango balls are grilled, brush them generously with the sweet soy sauce glaze.
12. Return the glazed dango skewers to the grill or broiler for another 1-2 minutes, or until the glaze caramelizes and becomes shiny.
13. Remove the Mitarashi Dango from the heat and serve them hot.

Enjoy your homemade Mitarashi Dango as a delightful sweet treat!

Tai Meshi (Sea Bream Rice)Korokke (Japanese Croquettes)

Ingredients:

- 3 large potatoes, peeled and cut into chunks
- 1 small onion, finely chopped
- 100g ground beef or pork (optional)
- Salt and pepper to taste
- 2 tablespoons butter
- 2 tablespoons milk
- 1 tablespoon soy sauce
- 1 tablespoon Worcestershire sauce
- 1 cup panko breadcrumbs
- Vegetable oil for frying
- All-purpose flour for dredging
- 1-2 eggs, beaten

Instructions:

1. Boil the potatoes in a pot of salted water until they are fork-tender, about 15-20 minutes. Drain well.
2. In a skillet, melt the butter over medium heat. Add the chopped onion and cook until softened.
3. If using ground meat, add it to the skillet with the onions and cook until browned. Season with salt and pepper to taste.
4. Mash the boiled potatoes in a large bowl. Add the cooked onion and meat mixture (if using), milk, soy sauce, and Worcestershire sauce. Mix until well combined.
5. Shape the potato mixture into flat patties, about 1/2 inch thick.
6. Set up a dredging station with three shallow bowls: one with flour, one with beaten eggs, and one with panko breadcrumbs.
7. Dredge each potato patty in flour, then dip it into the beaten eggs, and finally coat it with panko breadcrumbs, pressing gently to adhere.
8. Heat vegetable oil in a deep skillet or frying pan over medium heat. Fry the korokke patties in batches until they are golden brown and crispy on both sides, about 3-4 minutes per side.
9. Remove the fried korokke patties from the oil and drain them on a paper towel-lined plate.

10. Serve the Potato Korokke hot, with tonkatsu sauce or Worcestershire sauce for dipping.

Enjoy your crispy and flavorful Japanese Croquettes as a tasty snack or side dish!

Gomaae (Sesame inach)

Ingredients:

- 1 bunch of fresh spinach, washed and trimmed
- 2 tablespoons sesame seeds
- 1 tablespoon soy sauce
- 1 tablespoon sugar
- 1 tablespoon mirin (Japanese sweet rice wine)
- 1 teaspoon sesame oil (optional)

Instructions:

1. Bring a pot of water to a boil. Add a pinch of salt.
2. Blanch the spinach in the boiling water for about 1-2 minutes, until wilted but still vibrant green.
3. Quickly transfer the blanched spinach to a bowl of ice water to stop the cooking process and preserve the color. Once cooled, drain the spinach and squeeze out excess water.
4. In a small skillet, toast the sesame seeds over medium heat until golden brown and fragrant, about 2-3 minutes. Be careful not to burn them.
5. Grind the toasted sesame seeds in a suribachi (Japanese mortar and pestle) or a spice grinder until finely ground. Alternatively, you can use a food processor or blender.
6. In a small bowl, combine the ground sesame seeds, soy sauce, sugar, mirin, and sesame oil (if using). Mix well to combine and dissolve the sugar.
7. Place the blanched spinach in a serving bowl. Pour the sesame sauce over the spinach.
8. Using your hands or tongs, gently toss the spinach with the sesame sauce until evenly coated.
9. Serve the Gomaae cold or at room temperature as a refreshing side dish.

Enjoy your homemade Gomaae with Spinach! It's a nutritious and flavorful addition to any Japanese meal.

Buta no Kakuni (Braised Pork Belly)

Ingredients:

- 1 kg (about 2.2 lbs) pork belly, skin removed and cut into large cubes
- 1 cup water
- 1 cup soy sauce
- 1 cup mirin (Japanese sweet rice wine)
- 1/2 cup sugar
- 2 cloves garlic, crushed
- 2 slices ginger
- 2 green onions, cut into large pieces
- Optional garnish: thinly sliced green onions, toasted sesame seeds

Instructions:

1. In a large pot or Dutch oven, combine the water, soy sauce, mirin, sugar, crushed garlic, ginger slices, and green onions. Stir to combine.
2. Add the pork belly cubes to the pot, making sure they are fully submerged in the liquid.
3. Bring the liquid to a boil over medium-high heat. Once boiling, reduce the heat to low and cover the pot with a lid.
4. Let the pork belly simmer gently for about 2-3 hours, or until it is very tender and easily pierced with a fork. Stir occasionally and check the liquid level to ensure the pork is always submerged. If needed, add more water to cover the pork.
5. Once the pork belly is tender, remove it from the pot and transfer it to a cutting board. Discard the ginger slices and green onions.
6. Increase the heat to medium-high and let the braising liquid boil until it reduces and thickens to a syrupy consistency, about 10-15 minutes.
7. While the braising liquid is reducing, you can optionally brown the pork belly cubes in a separate skillet to add more color and flavor.
8. Once the braising liquid has thickened, return the pork belly cubes to the pot and coat them with the sauce.
9. Serve the Buta no Kakuni hot, garnished with thinly sliced green onions and toasted sesame seeds if desired.

Enjoy your homemade Buta no Kakuni! It's a comforting and flavorful dish that pairs well with steamed rice and some pickled vegetables.

Yaki Udon (Stir-Fried Udon Noodles)

Ingredients:

- 200g udon noodles (fresh or dried)
- 1 tablespoon vegetable oil
- 2 cloves garlic, minced
- 1 small onion, thinly sliced
- 1 carrot, julienned
- 1 bell pepper, thinly sliced
- 1 cup cabbage, thinly sliced
- 100g protein of your choice (sliced chicken, beef, shrimp, tofu, etc.)
- 2-3 tablespoons soy sauce
- 1 tablespoon oyster sauce
- 1 tablespoon mirin (Japanese sweet rice wine)
- 1 teaspoon sesame oil
- Salt and pepper to taste
- Optional toppings: sliced green onions, sesame seeds, shredded nori seaweed

Instructions:

1. Cook the udon noodles according to the package instructions until they are al dente. Drain the noodles and rinse them under cold water to stop the cooking process. Set aside.
2. In a large skillet or wok, heat the vegetable oil over medium-high heat. Add the minced garlic and sauté for about 30 seconds, or until fragrant.
3. Add the sliced onion to the skillet and cook until softened.
4. Add the julienned carrot, sliced bell pepper, and thinly sliced cabbage to the skillet. Stir-fry the vegetables until they are tender-crisp.
5. Push the vegetables to one side of the skillet and add the protein (chicken, beef, shrimp, tofu, etc.) to the empty side. Cook until the protein is cooked through.
6. Add the cooked udon noodles to the skillet, along with the soy sauce, oyster sauce, mirin, and sesame oil. Toss everything together until well combined.
7. Continue to stir-fry the Yaki Udon for a few more minutes, allowing the noodles to absorb the flavors of the sauce and the ingredients to heat through.
8. Season with salt and pepper to taste, if needed.

9. Once everything is heated through and well mixed, remove the skillet from the heat.
10. Serve the Yaki Udon hot, garnished with sliced green onions, sesame seeds, and shredded nori seaweed if desired.

Enjoy your homemade Yaki Udon as a satisfying and flavorful noodle dish! Feel free to customize it with your favorite vegetables and proteins.

Kakiage (Mixed Vegetable Tempura)

Ingredients:

- Assorted vegetables (such as carrots, onions, bell peppers, sweet potatoes, zucchini, mushrooms, green beans, etc.), thinly sliced or julienned
- Optional: shrimp, squid, or other seafood, thinly sliced
- 1 cup all-purpose flour
- 1 tablespoon cornstarch
- 1 cup ice-cold water
- Vegetable oil for deep-frying
- Tempura dipping sauce (Tentsuyu), for serving

Instructions:

1. Prepare the vegetables and seafood by thinly slicing or julienning them into uniform pieces. Pat them dry with paper towels to remove excess moisture.
2. In a mixing bowl, combine the all-purpose flour and cornstarch. Gradually add the ice-cold water to the flour mixture, stirring gently with chopsticks or a fork until just combined. The batter should be lumpy and slightly thin.
3. Heat vegetable oil in a deep fryer or a large pot to 350°F (180°C).
4. Working in batches, dip a small handful of the prepared vegetables and/or seafood into the tempura batter, making sure they are evenly coated.
5. Carefully lower the battered vegetables and seafood into the hot oil, one by one. Fry them for 2-3 minutes, or until they are golden brown and crispy.
6. Use a slotted spoon or wire skimmer to remove the cooked kakiage from the oil, allowing any excess oil to drain off.
7. Transfer the cooked kakiage to a wire rack set over a baking sheet to keep them crispy while you fry the remaining batches.
8. Once all the kakiage is fried, serve them hot with tempura dipping sauce (Tentsuyu) on the side for dipping.
9. Enjoy your homemade Kakiage as a delicious appetizer or side dish!

You can customize your Kakiage with your favorite vegetables and seafood, and feel free to experiment with different dipping sauces for added flavor.

Ankake Yakisoba (Yakisoba Noodles with Thick Sauce)

Ingredients:

For the Yakisoba Noodles:

- 300g yakisoba noodles (fresh or dried)
- 1 tablespoon vegetable oil
- 1 small onion, thinly sliced
- 1 carrot, julienned
- 1 bell pepper, thinly sliced
- 100g cabbage, thinly sliced
- 100g thinly sliced pork belly or chicken breast (optional)
- Salt and pepper to taste

For the Ankake Sauce:

- 1 1/2 cups dashi stock (you can use instant dashi granules or make your own from kombu and bonito flakes)
- 2 tablespoons soy sauce
- 1 tablespoon mirin (Japanese sweet rice wine)
- 1 tablespoon oyster sauce
- 1 tablespoon cornstarch
- 2 tablespoons water

Instructions:

1. If using dried yakisoba noodles, cook them according to the package instructions until they are al dente. If using fresh yakisoba noodles, blanch them in boiling water for 1-2 minutes, then drain and rinse under cold water to stop the cooking process. Set aside.
2. In a small bowl, mix together the cornstarch and water to make a slurry. Set aside.
3. In a large skillet or wok, heat the vegetable oil over medium-high heat. Add the thinly sliced onion and cook until softened.

4. Add the julienned carrot, thinly sliced bell pepper, and thinly sliced cabbage to the skillet. Stir-fry the vegetables until they are tender-crisp.
5. If using thinly sliced pork belly or chicken breast, add it to the skillet with the vegetables and cook until it is cooked through.
6. Add the cooked yakisoba noodles to the skillet and toss everything together until well combined. Season with salt and pepper to taste.
7. In a separate saucepan, combine the dashi stock, soy sauce, mirin, and oyster sauce. Bring the mixture to a simmer over medium heat.
8. Once the sauce is simmering, gradually whisk in the cornstarch slurry. Cook, stirring constantly, until the sauce thickens to your desired consistency.
9. Pour the thickened ankake sauce over the yakisoba noodles and vegetables in the skillet. Gently toss everything together until the noodles are evenly coated with the sauce.
10. Once everything is heated through and well mixed, remove the skillet from the heat.
11. Serve the Ankake Yakisoba hot, garnished with thinly sliced green onions or toasted sesame seeds if desired.

Enjoy your homemade Ankake Yakisoba with its rich and flavorful thick sauce!

Kinpira Gobo (Braised Burdock Root)

Ingredients:

- 2 burdock roots (gobo), about 300g each
- 1 carrot, about 150g
- 2 tablespoons vegetable oil
- 2 tablespoons soy sauce
- 1 tablespoon mirin (Japanese sweet rice wine)
- 1 tablespoon sugar
- 1 teaspoon sesame oil
- Toasted sesame seeds for garnish (optional)
- Thinly sliced green onions for garnish (optional)

Instructions:

1. Peel the burdock roots and cut them into matchstick-sized strips. Immediately soak the cut burdock strips in a bowl of water to prevent discoloration.
2. Peel the carrot and cut it into matchstick-sized strips similar in size to the burdock strips.
3. In a large skillet or frying pan, heat the vegetable oil over medium heat. Add the drained burdock strips and carrots to the skillet and stir-fry for 3-4 minutes until they start to soften.
4. In a small bowl, mix together the soy sauce, mirin, sugar, and sesame oil until well combined.
5. Pour the soy sauce mixture over the burdock and carrots in the skillet. Stir well to coat the vegetables evenly.
6. Cover the skillet and simmer the vegetables over medium-low heat for about 15-20 minutes, stirring occasionally, or until the burdock and carrots are tender and the liquid has reduced to a glaze.
7. Once the vegetables are cooked and the sauce has thickened, remove the skillet from the heat.
8. Transfer the Kinpira Gobo to a serving dish and garnish with toasted sesame seeds and thinly sliced green onions if desired.
9. Serve the Kinpira Gobo hot or at room temperature as a delicious side dish or topping for rice.

Enjoy your homemade Kinpira Gobo with its delightful combination of flavors and textures!

Yudofu (Hot Tofu)

Ingredients:

- 1 block (about 14-16 ounces) of firm tofu
- 4 cups dashi stock (you can use instant dashi granules or make your own from kombu and bonito flakes)
- 2 tablespoons soy sauce
- 1 tablespoon mirin (Japanese sweet rice wine)
- 2 green onions, thinly sliced (optional)
- Grated ginger for serving (optional)

Instructions:

1. Cut the block of tofu into thick slices or cubes, depending on your preference.
2. In a large pot, combine the dashi stock, soy sauce, and mirin. Bring the mixture to a gentle simmer over medium heat.
3. Carefully add the tofu slices or cubes to the simmering broth. Be gentle to avoid breaking the tofu.
4. Allow the tofu to simmer in the broth for about 10-15 minutes, or until it is heated through and has absorbed some of the flavors of the broth.
5. Once the tofu is heated through, ladle the Yudofu into individual serving bowls, making sure to distribute the tofu evenly.
6. Garnish the Yudofu with thinly sliced green onions and grated ginger if desired.
7. Serve the Yudofu hot as a comforting and nourishing dish.

Yudofu is often enjoyed with a dipping sauce made from soy sauce and grated ginger or with a drizzle of ponzu sauce. It's also delicious when served with a side of steamed rice and perhaps some pickled vegetables. Enjoy your homemade Yudofu!

Saba Shioyaki (Grilled Mackerel with Salt)

Ingredients:

- 2 whole mackerel, cleaned and gutted
- Salt
- Lemon wedges for serving (optional)

Instructions:

1. Preheat your grill to medium-high heat. If you don't have a grill, you can use a grill pan or broiler.
2. Score the skin of the mackerel on both sides with a sharp knife. This helps the fish cook more evenly and allows the salt to penetrate.
3. Pat the mackerel dry with paper towels to remove any excess moisture.
4. Sprinkle salt generously on both sides of the mackerel, rubbing it into the skin and flesh.
5. Once the grill is hot, place the mackerel directly on the grill grates. Alternatively, if using a grill pan or broiler, place the mackerel on a lightly greased pan.
6. Grill the mackerel for about 5-6 minutes on each side, or until the skin is crispy and the flesh is opaque and cooked through. The cooking time may vary depending on the thickness of the fish.
7. Once the mackerel is cooked, remove it from the grill and transfer it to a serving plate.
8. Serve the Saba Shioyaki hot, garnished with lemon wedges if desired.

Saba Shioyaki is often enjoyed with steamed rice and a side of vegetables or pickles. It's a simple yet delicious dish that highlights the natural flavors of the mackerel. Enjoy your homemade Saba Shioyaki!

Nasu Dengaku (Grilled Eggplant with Miso Glaze)

Ingredients:

- 2 medium-sized Japanese eggplants (or regular eggplants), sliced lengthwise
- 2 tablespoons white miso paste
- 1 tablespoon mirin (Japanese sweet rice wine)
- 1 tablespoon sugar
- 1 tablespoon sake (Japanese rice wine)
- 1 teaspoon sesame oil
- Optional garnish: toasted sesame seeds, thinly sliced green onions, shredded nori seaweed

Instructions:

1. Preheat your grill to medium-high heat. If you don't have a grill, you can use a grill pan or broiler.
2. Score the flesh of the eggplant slices in a criss-cross pattern to help absorb the flavors of the miso glaze.
3. In a small bowl, mix together the white miso paste, mirin, sugar, sake, and sesame oil until well combined.
4. Place the eggplant slices on the grill or grill pan. Grill them for about 3-4 minutes on each side, or until they are tender and have grill marks.
5. Once the eggplant is cooked, brush the miso glaze generously on one side of each slice.
6. Return the glazed eggplant slices to the grill or grill pan, glazed side down. Grill for another 1-2 minutes, or until the glaze caramelizes and becomes slightly charred.
7. Carefully flip the eggplant slices and brush the remaining miso glaze on the other side. Grill for another 1-2 minutes until the glaze is caramelized and bubbly.
8. Remove the Nasu Dengaku from the grill and transfer them to a serving plate.
9. Sprinkle toasted sesame seeds, thinly sliced green onions, or shredded nori seaweed on top for garnish if desired.
10. Serve the Nasu Dengaku hot as a delicious appetizer or side dish.

Enjoy your homemade Nasu Dengaku with its rich and flavorful miso glaze! It's a wonderful way to enjoy the natural sweetness of eggplant with a savory twist.

Gyu Don (Beef and Onion Rice Bowl)

Ingredients:

- 300g thinly sliced beef (such as ribeye or sirloin)
- 2 onions, thinly sliced
- 3 tablespoons soy sauce
- 3 tablespoons mirin (Japanese sweet rice wine)
- 2 tablespoons sake (Japanese rice wine)
- 1 tablespoon sugar
- 1 cup dashi stock (you can use instant dashi granules or make your own from kombu and bonito flakes)
- 2 cups cooked Japanese short-grain rice
- Optional garnish: thinly sliced green onions, toasted sesame seeds, pickled ginger

Instructions:

1. In a large skillet or frying pan, combine the soy sauce, mirin, sake, sugar, and dashi stock. Bring the mixture to a simmer over medium heat.
2. Add the thinly sliced onions to the skillet and cook them in the simmering liquid for about 5 minutes, or until they are softened.
3. Add the thinly sliced beef to the skillet, spreading it out evenly over the onions. Let the beef cook for about 2-3 minutes, or until it is no longer pink.
4. Once the beef is cooked, stir everything together to combine and let it simmer for another 1-2 minutes to allow the flavors to meld.
5. Taste the Gyudon sauce and adjust the seasoning if necessary. You can add more soy sauce, mirin, or sugar according to your taste preference.
6. Once the Gyudon is ready, divide the cooked rice among serving bowls.
7. Using a slotted spoon, top each bowl of rice with the beef and onion mixture, making sure to evenly distribute the meat and onions.
8. Optionally, garnish each bowl of Gyudon with thinly sliced green onions, toasted sesame seeds, or pickled ginger for added flavor and texture.
9. Serve the Gyudon hot and enjoy!

Gyudon is a comforting and satisfying meal that's perfect for lunch or dinner. It's quick and easy to make at home and sure to be a hit with your family and friends.

Tamagoyaki (Japanese Rolled Omelette)

Ingredients:

- 4 large eggs
- 2 tablespoons mirin (Japanese sweet rice wine)
- 1 tablespoon soy sauce
- 1 teaspoon sugar
- 1/4 teaspoon salt
- Vegetable oil for cooking

Instructions:

1. In a bowl, whisk together the eggs, mirin, soy sauce, sugar, and salt until well combined.
2. Heat a Tamagoyaki pan or a square-shaped frying pan over medium heat. Brush the pan with a thin layer of vegetable oil.
3. Pour a thin layer of the egg mixture into the pan, just enough to cover the bottom. Tilt the pan to spread the egg mixture evenly.
4. Once the bottom of the egg has set but the top is still slightly runny, use chopsticks or a spatula to roll the egg from one side of the pan to the other, creating a thin layer.
5. Push the rolled egg to one side of the pan and brush the empty side with a little more oil. Pour another thin layer of the egg mixture into the empty side of the pan, lifting the rolled egg slightly to allow the new layer to flow underneath.
6. Once the new layer of egg has set slightly, roll it up together with the existing roll, starting from the side with the previously rolled egg.
7. Repeat this process, adding more layers of egg and rolling them up until you have used all of the egg mixture.
8. Once the Tamagoyaki is fully rolled and cooked through, transfer it to a cutting board.
9. Let the Tamagoyaki cool for a few minutes before slicing it into rounds.
10. Serve the Tamagoyaki slices hot or at room temperature as a delicious side dish or topping for sushi rice.

Enjoy your homemade Tamagoyaki! It's a classic Japanese dish that's perfect for breakfast, lunch, or as a snack.

Matcha Latte

Ingredients:

- 1 teaspoon matcha powder
- 2 tablespoons hot water (not boiling)
- 1 cup milk (dairy or plant-based)
- Sweetener of your choice (such as honey, sugar, or maple syrup), to taste (optional)

Instructions:

1. Sift the matcha powder into a cup or bowl to break up any clumps.
2. Add the hot water to the matcha powder and whisk vigorously until the mixture is smooth and frothy. You can use a traditional bamboo whisk (chasen) or a small whisk.
3. In a small saucepan, heat the milk over medium heat until it's hot but not boiling. Alternatively, you can heat the milk in the microwave.
4. Pour the hot milk into the matcha mixture and stir well to combine.
5. If desired, sweeten your Matcha Latte with honey, sugar, or maple syrup, adjusting the amount to taste.
6. Pour the Matcha Latte into a mug and enjoy!

You can also customize your Matcha Latte by adding a sprinkle of matcha powder or cinnamon on top for garnish. Feel free to experiment with different types of milk or sweeteners to suit your preferences. Enjoy your homemade Matcha Latte!

www.ingramcontent.com/pod-product-compliance
Lightning Source LLC
LaVergne TN
LVHW081610060526
838201LV00054B/2179